Three Simple Rules

Leader Guide

ABINGDON PRESS
NASHVILLE

THREE SIMPLE RULES 24/7
LEADER GUIDE

Edited by Josh Tinley
Cover Design by Marcia C'deBaca

Copyright © 2008 by Abingdon Press

All rights reserved. No part of this work may be reproduced or transmitted in any form or by any means, electronic or mechanical, including photocopying and recording, or by any information or retrieval system, except as may be expressly permitted in the 1976 Copyright Act or in writing from the publisher. Requests for permission should be addressed in writing to Permissions Office, P. O. Box 801, 201 Eighth Avenue, South, Nashville, Tennessee 37202-0801, or call 615- 749-6421.

Scripture quotations in this publication unless otherwise indicated, are from the New Revised Standard Version of the Bible, copyright © 1989 by the Division of Christian Education of the National Council of the Churches of Christ in the United States of America, and are used by permission. All rights reserved.

ISBN-13: 978-1-426-700347

Manufactured in the United States of America

10 11 12 13 14 15 16 17—10 9 8 7 6 5

CONTENTS

Introduction 4

Rule 1: Do No Harm

Introduction 7

Session 1 10

Session 2 15

Rule 2: Do Good

Introduction 20

Session 3 23

Session 4 28

Rule 3: Stay in Love With God

Introduction 33

Session 5 36

Session 6 42

Intergenerational Worship 47

Three Simple Rules
Introduction

This study was inspired by the book *Three Simple Rules: A Wesleyan Way of Living,* by Rueben P. Job. The three rules to which the book refers are the General Rules that John Wesley wrote as part of his instructions to early Methodist societies in England: Do no harm, do good, and attend to the ordinances of God (in Job's words, "Stay in love with God").

Rueben Job, in the preface to Three Simple Rules, boldly asserts that these three rules "have the power to change the world." The power of these rules lies largely in their simplicity. Clergy, scholars, theologians, and ethicists devote lifetimes to studying and interpreting the hundreds of commandments found in the Bible and the countless standards that have resulted from two millennia of church tradition. For many people, the seemingly simple goal of living a Christian life becomes complicated and confusing.

The Holy Club

Three Simple Rules: Introduction

The three simple rules to do no harm, do good, and stay in love with God get at the essence of the Christian faith: loving God and loving our neighbor as ourselves. Job describes these three rules as a blueprint for Christian living that are "accessible and inviting to young and old, rich and poor, powerful and weak, and those of every theological persuasion." He adds that, "At their best, Christians believe that such a way of living exists and is open to all."

As people adopt this way of living, they will become more compassionate, find more productive ways to resolve conflicts, work to correct injustices, grow in their relationship with Christ, and strive to better know God's will for their lives. In other words, following these three simple rules brings the world in line with the vision of God's kingdom that we find in Scripture.

Youth and the Three Simple Rules

When he wrote his three General Rules, John Wesley gave several examples of situations in which the rules would apply. He lists "doing ordinary work" on the "day of the Lord," "unprofitable conversation," and "putting on ... costly apparel" as ways of doing harm; he names feeding the hungry, visiting the sick and imprisoned, and taking up our cross daily as ways to do good; and he tells us to stay in love with God through public worship, family and private prayer, and fasting or abstinence (among others).

The language that Wesley uses and many of the examples that he gives may seem odd to youth who have been raised in a post-Christian culture. Many people today don't think twice about doing "ordinary work" on the sabbath and see nothing wrong with wearing "costly apparel." Taking up their cross may be a strange concept for teens who have been raised to expect comfort and convenience. Families who are always on the go rarely have time to stop and pray together; and the practices of fasting and abstinence largely have been relegated to programs such as 30-Hour Famine and True Love Waits.

On the other hand, the millennial generation (people born between 1982 and 1999, give or take a few years) has shown an eagerness to change the world in positive ways. Teens today are not averse to making sacrifices on behalf of others, to eliminating practices and habits that are harmful, or to engaging in spiritual practices. They want to do no harm, do good, and stay in love with God; but they need adults to guide and set an example for them. It is hoped that this study will help youth discover ways that they can have a positive impact on the world around them by making these three simple rules part of their lives.

Teaching Three Simple Rules 24/7

The goal of this study is to get youth to think critically about their attitudes and behaviors. Rather than getting caught up in specific ways of doing good or not doing harm, you should encourage the youth to adopt a do-good, do-no-harm attitude. Youth shouldn't come away from these six sessions with a list of dos and don'ts; they should, instead, come away with a sense of how to apply the three simple rules to their daily lives and the situations they encounter.

The six sessions in this study are divided into three, two-session units: one unit for each of the three simple rules. The first session in each unit focuses on the rule itself and helps youth understand the concept of doing no harm, doing good, or staying in love with God. These sessions look at the rule as John Wesley wrote it as well as Rueben Job's interpretation of the rule as stated in *Three Simple Rules*. The activities in these sessions are geared toward helping youth better understand the meaning of each rule.

The second session in each unit focuses on how the youth can apply the rule to their lives. The activities in these sessions look at opportunities that young people have to do no harm, do good, and stay in love with God and demonstrate the positive effects of being faithful to these rules.

Weekly Challenges and Optional Reading Assignments

Five of the six sessions conclude with a "Weekly Challenge" that gives participants a way to practice what they have learned during the week between sessions. These challenges allow the youth to experience the rules they are learning about.

The first session in each unit also includes an optional Reading Assignment that asks youth to read a chapter of Three Simple Rules in the coming week and to reflect on a few questions as they read. Groups who choose to do these assignments can debrief, in the second session of each unit, what they have read.

Do No Harm
Introduction

The Rule

Few would dispute the simplicity of the first simple rule. Rules don't get much more straight-forward than "Don't do bad things." Staying faithful to this rule, however, is anything but simple. For one, following the rule to do no harm involves following several other rules. John Wesley wrote a great deal about these rules-within-the-rule, giving his readers a litany of examples of doing harm, including:

- Taking God's name in vain
- Not keeping the sabbath
- Fighting
- Gossip and slander
- Spending money on luxuries that we don't need.
- Wasting our time doing things that "do not tend to the knowledge or love of God"

(See John Wesley's entire list of examples on pages 6–7 of the student book.)

Wesley challenged those in his Methodist societies to avoid "evil of every kind, especially that which is most generally practiced." In other words, it wasn't enough to avoid behaviors that everyone agreed were bad (murder, adultery, and such); Wesley wanted the Methodists to also avoid sinful behaviors that had become largely acceptable in their culture.

Each of us knows of groups that are locked in conflict, sometimes over profound issues and sometimes over issues that are just plain silly. But the conflict is real, the divisions deep, and the consequences can often be devastating. If, however, all who are involved can agree to do no harm, the climate in which the conflict is going on is immediately changed. How is it changed? Well, if I am to do no harm, I can no longer speak gossip about the conflict. I can no longer speak disparagingly about those involved in the conflict. I can no longer manipulate the facts of the conflict. I can no longer diminish those who do not agree with me and must honor each as a child of God. I will guard my lips, my mind and my heart so that my language will not disparage, injure or wound another child of God. I must do no harm, even while I seek a common good.

—**Rueben Job,** *Three Simple Rules,* p. 22

Youth and The Rule

Many teens, having been raised in a post-Christian consumer culture, would not even recognize some of the examples in Wesley's list as ways of doing harm. Taking God's name in vain, working on the sabbath, and buying things we don't need have become so acceptable in our culture that avoiding such behavior takes a lot of effort.

Rather than focus on the individual ways of doing harm that John Wesley identified, youth should work to adopt a "do no harm" attitude, in which they continually assess whether their actions are having a negative affect on their relationships with God and others. Before passing on a juicy rumor, youth should think about whom could be hurt or whose trust might be betrayed. Before skipping worship or youth group to pursue another opportunity, youth should consider their commitment to God and their Christian community. And before making a frivolous purchase, youth should think about how the money they would spend could be put to better use.

Doing no harm will no doubt be inconvenient (not buying products made with child labor) or off-putting (refusing to retaliate after being insulted) at times, but the benefits are worth the effort. Resisting the urge to do harm creates a climate where respect and compassion can flourish and where rage and regret have no place.

Rule 1: Do No Harm, Introduction

Teaching These Sessions

Rule 1: Do No Harm, Part 1

This first session introduces youth to the three simple rules, focusing specifically on the first rule. The purpose of this lesson is for youth to get a sense of what John Wesley meant when he instructed people in his societies to "do no harm." The youth will read Wesley's original rendering of the rule, discuss an excerpt from *Three Simple Rules,* by Rueben Job (the book on which this study is based), study Scriptures related to this rule, and experience a method of conflict resolution that represents one of many ways to obey this rule. The session ends with a worship experience: the celebration of a love feast.

As you teach, focus on what it means to do harm, the consequences of doing harm, and the benefits of being faithful to this rule. Also emphasize that, when Wesley tells us to "do no harm," he means that we should do no harm to anyone, regardless of how much we may dislike a person and regardless of what harm anyone has done to us.

Rule 1: Do No Harm, Part 2

The second session moves into applying the first rule to one's day-to-day life. The youth will look at ways of doing harm that are relevant to their lives; they will study Mark 4:30-32 (the parable of the mustard seed) and Galatians 5:9 ("A little yeast leavens the whole batch of dough") as illustrations of how a small group of people committed to doing no harm can have a world-changing effect. The youth will read an excerpt from *Three Simple Rules* that explains what a commitment to doing no harm on a daily basis entails.

When you teach this lesson, focus on the example that we set by doing no harm. What can people learn from our way of living about God's will for the world? Challenge the youth to think about the example they set by their day-to-day decisions to do no harm.

Basic Supplies for This Study

The following supplies will be used frequently throughout this study, so they will not be listed in the supplies for each activity:

- Bibles
- Student books
- Paper
- Pens or pencils
- Markerboard and/or large sheets of paper
- Broad-tip markers
- Copy of *Three Simple Rules,* by Rueben Job, for each youth (optional)

Session 1

Rule 1: Do No Harm
Part 1

Theme: Doing no harm, in theory

Key Scripture: "You have heard that it was said, 'You shall love your neighbor and hate your enemy.' But I say to you, Love your enemies and pray for those who persecute you" (Matthew 5:43-44).

Three Simple Rules

As the youth arrive, say: "The Bible has hundreds of commandments and teachings that deal with how we should live. Throughout the history of the church, as culture and technology have posed new questions and challenges, Christians have applied the teachings of Scripture to come up with rules of living for their place and time. Rather than trying to name these hundreds of laws and commandments, we're going to come up with three big rules that cover everything."

Divide the youth into groups of 3 or 4, and challenge each group to come up with three rules that summarize all of the laws and commandments from the Bible and Christian tradition. Give the groups about five minutes to work, then ask each group to read aloud its three rules. Record all of the rules on a markerboard. If time permits, work together to narrow the list to three rules that the class can agree on.

Do No Harm

Say: "John Wesley, the founder of Methodism, was a pastor in the Church of England in the 1700s. He organized 'Methodist Societies' for people in the church who were serious about being holy and maturing as Christians. He demanded that members of these societies follow three General Rules: 1) do no harm; 2) do good; and 3) stay in love with God. For the first two sessions of this study, we're going to focus on the first rule, 'Do no harm.' "

Rule 1: Do No Harm, Part 1

Ask the youth to turn to pages 6 and 7 in the student book and to read the first General Rule as it appears in *The Book of Discipline of The United Methodist Church*. (You might choose to have a volunteer read it aloud while the others follow along.) Point out the notes that have been included to clarify some of John Wesley's wording.

Then have everyone turn to page 8 in the student book and work through the following activity individually:

John Wesley gives several examples of what he means by "Do no harm." Look over these examples again on pages 6–7. Circle the ones that you think apply to Christians in today's world. Cross out the ones that you think no longer apply to us. If you are unsure of the meaning of one of Wesley's examples, leave it as is.

- What is harmful about each of John Wesley's examples of doing harm?
- Look over the items you have circled. Which of these ways of doing harm are difficult for you to avoid? Why?
- Count the items that you crossed out. For each one you have crossed out, replace it with an example of doing harm that better applies to Christians today. (For instance, if you crossed out five items, come up with five new examples of doing harm that we should avoid.)

Give the youth plenty of time to work, then ask volunteers to tell which items they crossed out and why. If the youth disagree on which items should be crossed out, allow the students to make a case for why a certain example is or is not relevant to our world today.

Then ask volunteers to name some of the new examples that they came up with. Record these on a large sheet of paper and keep them handy for next week.

Peacemakers

Ask a youth to read aloud the excerpt from *Three Simple Rules* on page 9 of the student book. Then ask the youth to compare the examples of doing no harm that Rueben Job names in this passage with those that John Wesley listed (see pages 6–7 of the student book) and with those that your group came up with (see "Do No Harm," above).

Point out that Job focuses mainly on relationships and going out of our way to avoid doing harm to other people. Then ask volunteers to read aloud the related Scriptures, Matthew 5:43-48 and Romans 12:14-18, on page 9 of the student book. After each Scripture is read, ask:

- What does this Scripture say about doing no harm, especially in our relationships with others?
- What is most challenging about this Scripture?

The Peace Rose

Say: "Rueben Job suggests that, by going out of our way to do no harm, we can keep our conflicts with other people from having devastating consequences."

Supplies
- Rose or another flower, real or artificial (If you use a real rose, take care that no one is hurt by its thorns.)

Direct the youth to the information about the Peace Rose on page 10 of the student book. Then invite the group to spend a few minutes brainstorming conflicts that are common among their friends and peers. These might include fights with siblings over borrowed clothing, clashes with parents over grades or priorities, and tensions among friends who have betrayed each other's trust. Once you have a pretty good list, ask the youth to narrow down the list to three or four conflicts that they think are especially interesting.

Rule 1: Do No Harm, Part 1

Then select a pair of volunteers to roleplay each conflict. Encourage the actors to really get into character, showing anger about the situation and leveling accusations against each other. Invite one pair at a time to act out its assigned conflict; then ask the pair to come to the Peace Rose to work out the dispute. Hand the rose to one person and allow him or her to explain his or her side of the story; when he or she is finished, have him or her hand the rose to the other person and allow that person to give his or her side of the story. Continue until the pair peacefully resolves the conflict. Repeat this process with the other conflicts.

Then ask:

- What makes the Peace Rose effective?
- In what situations, if any, might the rose be ineffective?
- How effective would the Peace Rose be if only one party were to take it seriously?
- How might this exercise help you resolve conflicts in situations where no Peace Rose is available?
- What does the Peace Rose have to do with John Wesley's rule to "do no harm"?

Explain to the youth that, by choosing to listen to and understand the person with whom you are in conflict, you are not allowing the conflict to escalate: You are making a conscious effort to avoid (or to put an end to) verbal and physical violence.

Love Feast

Ask a volunteer to read aloud the excerpt from *Three Simple Rules* on page 11 of the student book. Emphasize the sentence in which Job says, "We discover that we stand on common ground, inhabit a common and precious space, share a common faith, feast at a common table, and have an equal measure of God's unlimited love."

Supplies
- Baskets of bread and finger foods
- Pitchers of ice water
- Cups, napkins, and plates

As an expression of the "common table" at which we all feast, hold a "love feast." A love feast is a Christian fellowship meal inspired by the meals that Jesus shared with his disciples and others during his earthly ministry.

Gather the youth around a table and set out baskets of bread and finger foods, along with pitchers of ice water. Set out plates, napkins, and cups; and pass around the baskets and pitcher.

Three Simple Rules 24/7

While the food is being passed around the table, have volunteers read aloud Scriptures that involve food and doing no harm, such as Romans 12:20a ("If your enemies are hungry, feed them; if they are thirsty, give them something to drink"); Leviticus 23:22 ("When you reap the harvest of your land, you shall not reap to the very edges of your field, or gather the gleanings of your harvest; you shall leave them for the poor and for the alien"); 1 Corinthians 11:18b, 21-22 (abuses during the Lord's supper). These examples can be found on page 11 of the student book.

When everyone has been served, ask a youth to read aloud the "Weekly Challenge" on page 12 of the student book. ("In the coming week avoid doing harm by making a commitment not to say anything negative about any other person.") Then have a time of prayer in which you pray that God would give everyone in the group the strength to do no harm.

Reading Assignment (Optional)

If possible, get one copy of *Three Simple Rules,* by Rueben Job, for each youth. Ask the youth in the coming week to read the chapter "Do No Harm" (pages 19–32). Tell them to think about the following questions as they read. (These are printed on page 12 of the student book).

- What are some ways that people do harm without even thinking about it?
- What is most challenging about practicing this rule to do no harm?
- How would your life be different if you were fully devoted to following this rule? How would our church, our community, and our nation be different if everyone were to take this rule seriously?

Session 2

Rule 1: Do No Harm
Part 2

Theme: Doing no harm, in practice

Key Scripture: A little yeast leavens the whole batch of dough (Galatians 5:9).

If You Don't Have Anything Nice to Say...

Beforehand, find the most ridiculous picture you can of a person dressed in gaudy 1970s fashion. Old department store catalogs or album covers would be a good place to look; there are also several appropriate images on the Internet.

Supplies
- Photo of someone from the 1970s who is dressed in gaudy clothing from the time

Post the image near a markerboard. As youth arrive, ask them to write on the markerboard the first words that come to mind that would describe the picture. Once almost everyone has arrived, review the words that they listed. If there are no negative or derogatory words, commend the group on being able to "do no harm."

If such words do appear on the list, remind the youth of their commitment from the week before to do no harm by not saying anything negative about other persons. Then ask the youth why they felt that it was OK to say negative things about the person in the picture. (Keep the discussion going by following up with questions such as, "Is insulting a nameless person in a photo less harmful than insulting someone you know?" "If most people agree that certain fashions from the 1970s were ugly, is it OK to poke fun at what somebody wore back then?")

Then ask:

- How well did you live up to the weekly challenge to do no harm by not saying negative things about others?

Three Simple Rules 24/7

- What was most difficult about this commitment? When were you most tempted to say something insulting?
- How did avoiding insults and negative comments affect your relationships with others?

Reading Assignment (Optional)

If your group did the optional reading assignment (the "Do No Harm" chapter of *Three Simple Rules*), open by asking the youth to give their impressions of the reading and to name some of the key points that the author, Rueben Job, makes in this chapter. Then discuss the questions below, which the youth were asked to reflect on:

- What are some ways that people do harm without even thinking about it?
- What is most challenging about following this rule to do no harm?
- How would your life be different if you were fully devoted to following this rule? How would our church, our community, and our nation be different if everyone were to take this rule seriously?

The 'Do No Harm' List

Direct the youth to the list of examples of doing harm that you created during the previous session. (See "Do No Harm," on pages 10–11.) For each example, ask:

- What is harmful about this action? Who is harmed?
- How difficult is it to avoid this type of doing harm? (You might have the youth answer this question on a scale from 1 to 5, with 1 being "easy" and 5 being "extremely difficult," by holding up the appropriate number of fingers.)

A New, Not-so-Harmful, World

Divide the youth into teams of 3 or 4, and assign each team one of the items from the list of examples of doing harm (above). Challenge each team to create a poster or a skit that imagines what your community or the world would be like if everyone could avoid harmful behavior. Give the teams plenty of time to work, then ask each team to present its work.

Rule 1: Do No Harm, Part 2

Tell the youth that Rueben Job begins the preface to *Three Simple Rules* by saying that these rules "have the power to change the world." Lift up the students' skits and posters as examples of how the first rule ("Do no harm") has the potential to change the world.

Say: "The only problem with these visions of a better world is that they depend on *everyone* making a commitment to do no harm and being faithful to this commitment. Since it is unlikely that all people will suddenly stop doing harm, how will this rule change the world?"

To answer this question, ask one youth to read aloud Mark 4:30-32 and another to read aloud Galatians 5:9. (Both are printed on page 13 of the student book.) If you have a youth who has had experience baking bread, invite him or her explain the role of yeast and how a small amount of yeast affects the quality and texture of an entire loaf of bread.

Explain that both of these Scriptures involve small things that have a big impact and that these Scriptures affirm that one person can make a difference. If one person makes a commitment to doing no harm, others will take notice: They'll notice a change in the person's attitude and behavior, and that attitude and behavior will rub off. Gradually, more and more people will adopt a "do no harm" lifestyle, and our community and world will change in significant ways. (This view may seem overly optimistic, but the optimism is supported by Scripture.)

Plant the Mustard; Be the Mustard

Supplies

Gather the following for each student:
- Mug or small flower pot
- Mustard seed
- Fertile garden soil
- Water

To bring the parable of the mustard seed (Mark 4:30-32) to life, have the youth plant mustard seeds. Give each youth a mug or small pot (or you might choose to ask the youth to bring an old coffee mug with them), some fertile garden soil, and a mustard seed.

Instruct the youth to fill their mugs or pots with the soil and to plant their seeds less than a centimeter beneath the surface of the soil. Then have the youth water the soil and put the mugs or or pots in a sunny window.

Then throughout the season, you and the youth will be able to watch the mustard plants grow. By the end of this study, you should see substantial results.

Option: If your church's property and trustees permit, plant the seeds outside. Plant them about three inches apart and water them generously. Mustard grows best in cool weather. Someone may need to check on the seeds on weekdays to make sure that they are getting enough water.

Unearned, Unlimited, and Undeserved

Say: "The hardest part of doing no harm is doing no harm even to people you don't like."

You might take this time to review the Scriptures on page 9 of the student book (Matthew 5:43-48 and Romans 12:14-18) about loving enemies.

Then ask a youth to read aloud the excerpt from *Three Simple Rules* printed on page 14 of the student book. Explain that God loves each of us, even though none of us has done anything to earn or deserve that love. We should follow God's example by loving others even if they have done nothing to earn or deserve it.

To emphasize this point, ask another volunteer to read aloud the statement from John Wesley ("See that you are courteous toward all [people]") on page 14 of the student book. Then point out that author Rueben Job also describes God's love as "unlimited." Ask:

- What does it mean for God's love to be unlimited?
- Are humans capable of unlimited love? Explain.

Rule 1: Do No Harm, Part 2

- What limits do we place on love? That is, what factors keep us from fully loving all people?
- What does unlimited love have to do with Wesley's rule to "do no harm"?

Say: "When we seek to follow God's example by showing unlimited love to all people—regardless of whether they have earned or deserved it—we are much less likely to do harm."

Then ask a youth to read aloud the Weekly Challenge on page 15 of the student book. Give the youth some time to reflect silently on the challenge and to commit to eliminating one particular way of doing harm that they struggle with.

Close in prayer, asking God's continued help and guidance in avoiding doing harm.

Do Good
Introduction

The Rule

The first rule is all about what we shouldn't do. While the benefits of doing no harm are obvious, we must be careful not to reduce our life of faith to a list of "don'ts." When we focus too much on what not to do, our faith becomes passive. Fortunately, the second simple rule, "Do good," is more active. In addition to avoiding bad things, we should seek out good things. As he did with examples of doing no harm, John Wesley provides a list of some of these good things:

- Feeding the hungry, caring for the sick, and reaching out to others in need
- Helping other members of the "household of faith"
- Being diligent and frugal
- Denying ourselves for Christ's sake

The church gives us several opportunities to obey the second simple rule. Many congregations organize mission trips and service projects, host dinners for those who are hungry or lonely, provide shelter for the homeless, and offer help to persons struggling with addiction. Most churches give members of the congregation opportunities to play leadership roles in these ministries or to serve the "household of faith" by participating in the church's music and education ministries. But doing good is by no means limited to activities organized by the church. Every hour of every day brings opportunities to do good through acts of compassion, kindness, and justice.

Rule 2: Do Good, Introduction

Doing good, like doing no harm, is a proactive way of living. I do not need to wait until circumstances cry out for aid to relieve suffering or correct some horrible injustice. I can decide that my way of living will come down on the side of doing good to all in every circumstance and in every way I can. I can decide that I will choose a way of living that nourishes goodness and strengthens community.
—**Rueben Job,** *Three Simple Rules,* pp. 37–38

Youth and the Rule

The millennial generation (young people born between 1982 and 1999, give or take a couple years) is known for its desire to change the world in positive ways. Many millennials are eager to serve others, to champion causes, and to find creative ways to improve their communities and the world. And the church, schools, and scouting organizations give youth several chances to effect change. The importance of doing good is nothing new to youth. But even those teens who seize every opportunity to serve others—who go on every mission trip and regularly volunteer to help younger students, serve food to the hungry, or spend time with older adults—can discover new ways to do good.

Youth need to see that doing good is not limited to service projects and volunteer hours. Challenge them to look for ways to do good in the hallway between classes at school, at home with their families, and even when they're in public surrounded by strangers. Encourage them to think of ways that they can do good for people who might not seem worthy of goodness. In other words, youth need to see how doing good can become a lifestyle.

Teaching These Sessions

Rule 2: Do Good, Part 1
Session 3 in this study introduces the second simple rule, "Do good." The primary objective of this lesson is for youth to get a sense of what John Wesley was talking about when he instructed those in his Methodist societies to do good. The students will read Wesley's original words as well as author Rueben Job's interpretation of this rule in his book *Three Simple Rules*. They will learn the importance of being proactive in doing good, and they will take part in a foot-washing activity.

As you teach this session, focus primarily on the concept of doing good, both by being proactive and by responding to circumstances. Encourage the youth to think about what makes an action good and about the difference between doing good and not doing bad.

Rule 2: Do Good, Part 2
Session 4 looks at the practice of doing good on a daily basis. Students will discuss their reasons for doing good and identify opportunities to do good in their lives at home, at school, and elsewhere. They will draw inspiration from Galatians 6:9-10 ("Let us not grow weary in doing what is right") and will learn to make a "careful and continual" assessment of their lives to ensure that they are being faithful to the second rule.

Use this session to encourage the youth to make doing good a habit and to look for opportunities to do good in all circumstances. Remind the youth that all people—even (and perhaps especially) enemies and strangers—are worthy recipients of acts of kindness and mercy.

Basic Supplies for This Study

The following supplies will be used frequently throughout this study, so they will not be listed in the supplies for each activity:

- Bibles
- Student books
- Paper
- Pens or pencils
- Markerboard and/or large sheets of paper
- Broad-tip markers
- Copy of *Three Simple Rules,* by Rueben Job, for each youth (optional)

Session 3

Rule 2: Do Good
Part 1

Theme: Doing good, in theory

Key Scripture: For we are what [God] has made us, created in Christ Jesus for good works, which God prepared beforehand to be our way of life (Ephesians 2:10).

If You Don't Have Anything Nice to Say...(Reprise)

As the youth arrive, ask them to think about the worst movie they've ever seen and the reasons they didn't like it. Once most youth have arrived and have had a little time to think, go around the room and invite each youth to name his or her least favorite movie and reasons for disliking it. Take note of any youth who is able to describe the worst movie he or she has ever seen without using language that is harmful or insulting. After everyone has had a chance to speak, congratulate those who were able to "do no harm" in their movie reviews. Then ask:

- Did you catch on that this activity was a test to see whether you could "do no harm" while talking about a bad movie?
- After spending two weeks talking about doing no harm, how hard was it to talk about a movie that you really didn't like?
- Does following the rule to "do no harm" mean not talking about movies, books, songs, or people we don't like? Explain.
- How can we give constructive criticism without being negative or harmful?

Then invite the youth to talk about the commitment they made for last week's "Weekly Challenge." Ask:

- How well did you live up to the weekly challenge to avoid one particular type of doing harm?
- What was most difficult about this commitment? When were you most tempted to break your commitment?

- How did avoiding this type of doing harm affect your relationships with others? with people whom you consider enemies?

Do Good

Ask the youth to turn to pages 16–17 in the student book and to read the second General Rule as it appears in *The Book of Discipline of The United Methodist Church*. (You might have a volunteer read it aloud while the others follow along.)

Then have everyone turn to page 18 in the student book.

Say: "As he did for the first rule, 'Do no harm,' John Wesley gives several examples of what he means by 'Do good.' Look over these examples on pages 16–17 of the student book. Circle the ones that you think apply to Christians in today's world. Cross out the ones that you think no longer apply to us. If you are unsure of the meaning of one of Wesley's examples, leave it as is." Ask:

- Look over the items you have circled. Which of these ways of doing good are difficult for you? Why?
- Look over the items you have crossed out. Why, do you think, are these ways of doing good no longer relevant?
- If Wesley were writing these rules today, what other examples of doing good might he add to the list?

Give the youth plenty of time to work, then ask volunteers to say which items they crossed out and why. If youth disagree on which items should be crossed out, allow them to make a case for why a certain example is or is not relevant to our world today.

Then ask volunteers to name some of the new examples that they came up with. Record these on a large sheet of paper and keep them for next week.

Proactive Goodness

Ask a youth to read aloud the excerpt from *Three Simple Rules* on page 18 of the student book. In this passage, Job talks about two kinds of doing good: responding to circumstances and being proactive.

Divide the youth into groups of 3 or 4 and have each group create two lists, one entitled "Responsive" and the other entitled "Proactive." The

Rule 2: Do Good

"Responsive" list should include examples of doing good that involve responding to situations, such as assisting a classmate who asks for help on a homework assignment or raising money to help victims of a recent natural disaster. The "Proactive" list should include examples of doing good without being prompted, such as performing random acts of kindness or volunteering to work with a ministry or organization that does good in the community.

Give the groups a few minutes to work, then ask each group to read aloud its lists. After each item is read, have members of the other groups raise their hands if they have listed the same item. Have the groups cross out any items that another group listed so that only the unique items remain. See which group listed the most unique examples of doing good responsively and which listed the most unique examples of doing good proactively. You might give a prize to the winning teams (although you should be clear that doing good should not be a competition).

Have the youth look back over the "Proactive" examples of doing good. Ask:

- Which of these things could you do or have you had the opportunity to do recently?
- What is most difficult about doing good without being asked or prompted?
- What are some small ways that you could do good every day so that being good would become a habit?

Then look at Ephesians 2:10, which is printed on page 19 of the student book. Ask:

- How does this Scripture relate to what author Rueben Job says in *Three Simple Rules*?
- How does knowing that you were "created for good works" affect how you live day-to-day?

All Day Long

Give each youth a sheet of paper and a pen or pencil. Instruct the youth to write, in fewer than 75 words, an account of their average day. (If the youth have trouble doing this, suggest that they choose one day of the week or an average day during a particular season.) Tell the youth to write in large letters so that their words take up most of the page.

Three Simple Rules 24/7

Allow a few minutes for the youth to write, then hand out sticky notes. Tell the youth to read through their accounts and identify opportunities to do good throughout their average day. For example, if they mention brushing their teeth, they could do good by turning off the water as they brush, thus saving a valuable resource that people need to live. At school, they may have opportunities to help peers with difficult subjects or to tutor younger students. They might also find several instances when they could simply be respectful or offer a kind word.

Supplies
- Several sticky notes for each youth

Have the youth write these opportunities to do good on the sticky notes and place the sticky notes on the appropriate spots on their papers. Invite volunteers to read aloud their accounts and the opportunities they identified.

Wash Those Feet!

One of Scripture's most memorable acts of doing good is Jesus' washing his disciples' feet. It was customary for a host to wash a guest's feet or for a servant to wash a master's feet. For a teacher to wash his students feet was truly remarkable.

Supplies
- Small clean towel for each youth
- Chair
- Basin
- Water enough for to fill the basin several times
- Wash cloth for each youth (optional)

Ask volunteers to read aloud John 13:1-17, 31-35, each person reading a few verses at a time. Have another volunteer read the material under "Wash Those Feet!" on page 19 of the student book.

Set out the chair and the basin of water and have the youth form a single-file line. Have the first person in line sit in the chair and remove his or her shoes and socks. Instruct the second person to wash and dry the first person's feet, using the water in the basin and one of the towels. (Be sure to tell the youth not to place their feet in the basin.) Then have the person who had washed the first person's feet sit down and remove his or her shoes and socks. Instruct the third person to wash the second person's feet. Continue until the final person in line is seated and barefoot, and have the first person wash the last person's feet.

If you or several of your youth aren't comfortable doing a foot-washing, another option would be to give shoulder rubs. In Jesus' day people's feet

Rule 2: Do Good

carried much of their stresses and burdens. Nowadays, we feel more stress in our back and neck areas.

After the foot-washing, ask a youth to read aloud the "Weekly Challenge" on page 19 of the student book. ("In the coming week, be on the lookout for ways to do good; and try to identify three ways that you can do good on a daily basis.") Then have a time of prayer in which you pray that God would give everyone the wisdom to see opportunities to do good in all circumstances.

Reading Assignment (Optional)

If each youth has a copy of *Three Simple Rules,* by Rueben Job, ask them in the coming week to read the chapter "Do Good" (pages 35–49). Tell the youth to think about the following questions as they read. (These are printed on page 20 of the student book).

- What is most challenging about practicing this rule to do good? Do you think that doing good is more or less difficult than not doing harm?
- Rueben Job mentions that our "gift of goodness may be rejected, ridiculed, and misused." When have you been rejected or ridiculed for doing good? How did you respond?
- What is the difference between healthy self-denial and unhealthy self-denial (page 45)? How can you practice healthy self-denial?
- How would your life be different if you were fully devoted to following this rule? How would your church, your community, and our nation be different if everyone took this rule seriously?

Session 4

Rule 2: Do Good
Part 2

Theme: Doing good, in practice

Key Scripture: So let us not grow weary in doing what is right, for we will reap at harvest-time, if we do not give up. So then, whenever we have an opportunity, let us work for the good of all, and especially those of the family of faith (Galatians 6:9-10).

What's Wrong With This Picture?

Beforehand, plant several opportunities to do good in and around your meeting space. You might scatter a few pieces of trash on the floor. You might invite an adult to wander around in the hallway outside your room as though he or she were looking for something. You could even set up a table featuring a picture of someone from your congregation who is away at college or serving overseas as a missionary, that person's name and address, some envelopes, and several pens and sheets of paper.

As the youth arrive, take note of which opportunities to do good they respond to and which they pass up. After most of the youth are present, ask:

- What opportunities to do good did you notice as you arrived this morning? Which of these opportunities did you respond to?

Point out any opportunities to do good that the youth didn't notice.

Then follow up on last week's "Weekly Challenge" by asking:

- What three examples of doing good every day did you identify?
- Which of these examples have you already put into practice?
- In the coming days and weeks, how could you do a better job of doing good in these ways?

Option: If you have *Veracity Video Vignettes, Volume 6,* (ISBN: 9780687465224), show the video "So You Call Yourself a Christian." Ask the youth to identify situations in the video that are opportunities to do good.

Rule 2: Do Good

Reading Assignment (Optional)

If your group did the optional reading assignment (the chapter "Do Good" in *Three Simple Rules*), open by asking the youth to give their impressions of the reading and to name some of the key points that author Rueben Job makes in this chapter. Then discuss the questions below, which the youth were asked to reflect on:

- What is most challenging about following this rule to do good? Do you think that doing good is more or less difficult than not doing harm?
- Rueben Job mentions that our "gift of goodness may be rejected, ridiculed, and misused." When have you been rejected or ridiculed for doing good? How did you respond?
- What is the difference between healthy self-denial and unhealthy self-denial (page 45)? How can you practice healthy self-denial?
- How would your life be different if you were fully devoted to following this rule? How would your church, your community, and our nation be different if everyone took this rule seriously?

Of Course, We Should Do Good

Ask a volunteer to read aloud the quotation from John Wesley on page 23 of the student book. You might suggest that youth memorize this quotation as a pithy reminder of the second general rule.

Say: "John Wesley's second General Rule is pretty obvious. Telling people that it's good to do good isn't exactly groundbreaking. But in reality, doing good is just as challenging as not doing harm."

Ask the youth to complete the activity on pages 21–22 in their student books by describing how they'd act in different hypothetical situations.

Give the youth plenty of time to work, then ask them to gather in the middle of the room. Explain that you will read aloud the scenarios from the student book and that the youth will indicate how they would act in that situation by moving to their left or to their right. The more confident they are in their answers, the farther to the left or right they should move. If they are unsure about an answer, they should stay closer to the middle.

Here are the hypothetical situations:

1. As you are riding your bike on a busy street, you notice a small turtle inching its way across the road.

- If you would stop your bike and move the turtle to safety, move to your right.
- If you would keep riding and leave the turtle to fend for itself, move to your left.

(Participants who would help the turtle without hesitation should move as far to the right as possible; participants who would help the turtle but would have reservations about taking the time or safety risk to do so would move only a few steps to their right.)

2. You have an opportunity to participate in an overseas mission trip, but going on the trip would mean that you would miss your seeing your favorite band in concert and celebrating your birthday at home.

    - If you would go on the trip anyway, move to your right.
    - If you would stay home, move to your left.

3. Your church is raising money for communities that were ravaged by a recent natural disaster. The only cash you have on hand is the money your aunt gave you for your birthday. You could donate your birthday money, but you already have big plans for how you would like to spend it.

    - If you would donate all of your birthday money, move to your right.
    - If you would keep all of your birthday money, move to your left.

4. You've just earned your driver's license. As you are driving, you notice a younger student from your school on the side of the road with a bicycle that obviously has a flat tire. You assume that he has a cell phone and has called someone, but you aren't sure.

    - If you were to stop to help him and offer him a lift, move to your right.
    - If you would keep driving, move to your left.

Add other examples that would resonate with your group.

Allow the youth to sit down. Then ask:

- What things did you have to sacrifice to do good in these situations? (*time, money, plans*)
- Why is it difficult to sacrifice these things?

Rule 2: Do Good

Remind the youth of your discussion of "proactive" and "responsive" ways of doing good from the previous session. Point out that all of the examples in this activity involved responding to circumstances; none involved being proactive. Ask the youth to name a few examples of doing good proactively. (These may be examples from the previous session or new ones that the youth have come up with.) After each example ask, "How might we have to sacrifice our time, our money, or our plans to do good in this way?"

Divide the youth into groups of 3 or 4. Instruct the groups to read the quotation from John Wesley and Galatians 6:9-10 (both of which are printed on page 23 of the student book) and to discuss the related questions on the same page.

For Goodness' Sake

Now that your group had discussed what it means to do good—and when, where, and how to do good—challenge the youth to think about why they should do good.

Ask the youth to spend a moment thinking about one act of good they did during the past week. Then ask them to think about why they did it.

Tell the youth to stand and gather into a circle. Toss a ball to one of the youth. When he or she catches the ball, ask him or her to name his or her act of good and the reason for doing it. Have this youth toss the ball to someone who hasn't had the ball. Continue until everyone has had a chance to speak.

Supplies
- Small ball

Then have the youth turn to Matthew 6:1-4 and ask a volunteer to read aloud this Scripture.

Say: "We shouldn't do good because we hope to be rewarded or recognized; we should do good because it's what God calls us to do."

A Careful and Continual Assessment

Ask a volunteer to read aloud the excerpt from *Three Simple Rules* on page 24 of the student book. In this passage, Rueben Job talks about making a "careful and continual assessment" of our lives and our world to ensure that we are faithfully doing good in all circumstances. He also writes of "seeking good for everyone," even those who hurt or offend us.

You might remind the youth of Matthew 5:43-48 ("Love your enemies") and Romans 12:14, 16-18 ("Bless those who persecute you"), both of which are printed on page 9 of the student book.

Then ask a youth to read aloud the "Weekly Challenge" on page 24 of the student book (a "careful and continual assessment" of the good they do and the good they neglect to do each day).

Say: "If we are going to do good to all people at all times, we have to remember that every person is worthy of our goodness."

Ask the youth to go around the room and say to each of their classmates, "You are worthy of my goodness."

Then close in prayer.

Stay in Love With God
Introduction

The Rule

One might argue that Wesley's third rule is an extension of his second rule. Staying in love with God is a very specific type of doing good. The third rule is also a reminder to us that successfully doing good and doing no harm requires us to stay connected with God, the source of all goodness.

John Wesley didn't actually use the wording "stay in love with God." That language comes from Rueben Job in his book *Three Simple Rules*. Wesley instead told his societies to "attend upon all the ordinances of God." He named the following as ordinances of God:

- Worship
- Reading or listening to the ministry of God's word
- Holy Communion
- Family and private prayer
- Bible study
- Fasting and abstinence

These ordinances are also known as spiritual disciplines or "means of grace" (to borrow a term from Wesley). These practices, among others (such as giving, witness, meditation, keeping the sabbath, and singing from the soul) help us stay focused on God and are ways that we open ourselves to God's grace.

> Living in the presence of and in harmony with the living God who is made known in Jesus Christ and companions us in the Holy Spirit is to live life from the inside out. It is to find our moral direction, our wisdom, our courage, our strength to live faithfully from the One who authored us, called us, sustains us, and sends us into the world as witnesses who daily practice the way of living with Jesus. Spiritual disciplines keep us in that healing, redeeming presence and power of God that forms and transforms each of us more and more into the image of the One we seek to follow.
> —**Rueben Job,** *Three Simple Rules,* p. 55

Youth and the Rule

In their landmark book *The Godbearing Life,* Kenda Creasy Dean and Ron Foster ask rhetorically, "How do we invite youth more deeply into the practices of faith?" The answer, they say, is "deceptively simple: We [those who lead youth] become more deeply involved in the practices of faith.... As we participate in the soul-shaping practices of faith, our life begins to look like Jesus' life."

The 2004 National Study of Youth and Religion found that a minority of religious teens practiced daily prayer and devotion. But young people aren't averse to spiritual disciplines. They just need some guidance. If we want youth to become fully engaged disciples of Christ, we need to give them examples of how to pray; provide resources and settings that will help them develop habits of devotion and Bible study; help them understand the significance of the sacraments; and introduce them to new practices that will help them connect with God, such as meditation or walking a labyrinth. We must also show youth how these disciplines change our life and make us more like Christ.

As the youth develop spiritual disciplines, they will be able to focus more clearly on God's will for their lives. They will become better equipped to overcome temptation, make difficult decisions, grow in their relationships with others, and cast their anxieties on God.

Rule 3: Stay in Love With God, Introduction

Teaching These Sessions

Rule 3: Stay in Love With God, Part 1

This session introduces students to the third and final rule, "Stay in love with God." The main objective of this session is to help youth understand what John Wesley was talking about when he told people to "attend to the ordinances of God" or "stay in love with God."

Youth will evaluate the spiritual disciplines that they already practice and how these disciplines bring them closer to God. They will also get a sense of how they might be faithful to Paul's command to "pray without ceasing."

As you teach this session, focus on spiritual disciplines as a means of grace and as a way to grow closer to God and to mature in faith.

Rule 3: Stay in Love With God, Part 2

The final session in this study looks at ways that youth can make spiritual disciplines an integral part of their daily lives. It looks at several spiritual habits named in Scripture, including Jesus' command to feed his sheep (a command that Rueben Job emphasizes in *Three Simple Rules*. Finally, this session challenges youth to identify concrete ways to apply what they've learned in this study in the coming days, weeks, and years.

When teaching this session, remind them that every moment is an opportunity to grow closer to God and that spiritual disciplines are not limited to prayer, worship, and Bible study.

Basic Supplies for This Study

The following supplies will be used frequently throughout this study, so they will not be listed in the supplies for each activity:

- Bibles
- Student books
- Paper
- Pens or pencils
- Markerboard and/or large sheets of paper
- Broad-tip markers
- Copy of *Three Simple Rules*, by Rueben Job, for each youth (optional)

Session 5

Rule 3: Stay in Love With God
Part 1

Theme: Staying in love with God, in theory

Key Scripture: Rejoice always, pray without ceasing, give thanks in all circumstances; for this is the will of God in Christ Jesus for you (1 Thessalonians 5:16-18).

Option: Wear your shirt inside out for this session.

Help, I'm Lost!

Arrange with a friend or family member who doesn't attend your church to help with this opening activity. Ask this person to wander the halls outside your meeting space as though he or she is lost. If a youth asks this person if he or she needs help, the person should say that he or she is looking for the church office or another location in your church building that the youth would know how to get to but that an outsider might have trouble finding. (If an adult approaches this person, he or she should just quietly say, "I'm helping with the youth Bible study.")

When most of the youth have arrived, check to see whether the person you recruited is still wandering the halls. Then explain that the whole situation was designed to give the youth an opportunity to do good. Discuss this activity by asking questions such as:

- Did you notice the person wandering the halls? If you did, did it cross your mind to offer to help this person?
- If you offered to help the person in the halls, why did you do so?
- What other opportunities to do good have you had in the past week? How did you respond in those situations? Why?

Then follow up on last week's "Weekly Challenge" by asking the youth whether they were able to faithfully keep a "Do Good Journal," recording both good things that they did and good things that they could have done.

Rule 3: Stay in Love With God

Ask:

- What did you learn by keeping this journal?
- Were you surprised by any of the ways in which you did good? Were you surprised by any of the opportunities you passed up?
- How did your attitude and/or behavior change as a result of doing this exercise?

Stay in Love With God

Be clear that, while obeying the first two rules is important to a Christian lifestyle, our salvation isn't determined by how many good things we do or how many bad things we don't do. Instead, we are saved by God's grace. And while God extends God's grace to all people in all situations, and while no one person gets more grace than any other person, certain practices help us experience God's grace more completely. Explain that those practices are at the heart of the third rule.

Ask the youth to turn to page 25 in the student book and to read the third General Rule as it appears in The Book of Discipline of The United Methodist Church. (You might choose to have a volunteer read it aloud while the others follow along.)

Then have everyone turn to page 26 in the student book.

Say: "List some ways in which you and/or your congregation practice each of the 'ordinances of God' that John Wesley names." (For example, students might write "Sunday morning worship" under "The public worship of God" or "blessing our meals" under "Family and private prayer.")

Give the youth plenty of time to work, then invite volunteers to talk about some of the things they listed. Add some examples of your own. Then ask:

- Which of the practices that you listed make you feel closest to God?
- Why, do you think, are these habits so important?
- Which of these things can be done individually? Which must be done as part of a Christian community?
- What do these habits have to do with staying in love with God?

Inside Out

Option: If you wore your shirt inside out for this session, tell the youth that they're about to learn why.

Ask a youth to read aloud the excerpt from *Three Simple Rules* on page 27 of the student book. Here Job talks about living life from the inside out, engaging in disciplines that transform our hearts, minds, and souls.

Tell the youth that spiritual disciplines have always been essential to Christian faith. Even Jesus, who was God in human form, spent time praying, fasting, and breaking bread with his disciples.

Ask a volunteer to read aloud Acts 2:41-42, which is printed on page 27 of the student book. Explain to the youth that this Scripture immediately follows the story of the first Christian Pentecost, the day when God poured out the Holy Spirit on Jesus' disciples and the day we recognize as the birthday of the church.

Say: "Immediately after the first believers joined the church, they devoted themselves to some of the spiritual disciplines that John Wesley later named in his General Rules and that we still practice today."

So What's the Point?

Say: "John Wesley often described spiritual practices such as prayer, Bible study, worship, and Holy Communion as 'means of grace.'"

If many of the youth have gone through confirmation in The United Methodist Church or another denomination with a Wesleyan heritage, ask them what they remember about grace from confirmation. You might remind them that John Wesley identified three types of grace: prevenient grace (the grace we receive from the day we are born that gently nudges us toward God), justifying grace (the grace enables us to experience and respond to God's love), and sanctifying grace (the grace through which we become more like Christ).

Say: "By definition, *grace* is something that God gives us, regardless of what we have done to deserve it. In fact, we cannot earn God's grace; it is a gift that God gives freely to all people. So what's the point of all of these 'means of grace'? If God's offers us grace no matter what, why should we bother with prayer, worship, and other spiritual practices?" (This is meant to be a rhetorical question, but allow the youth to answer if they have ideas.)

Rule 3: Stay in Love With God

To illustrate means of grace, ask the youth to stand up and to give themselves plenty of room.

Say: "Imagine that you are standing in a heavy rain and don't want to get wet. What might you do to avoid getting soaked?"

The youth might hunch their shoulders and put their hands over their head; if they're wearing a jacket, they might use it to cover as much of their bodies as possible.

Then say: "Imagine that you are standing in the same heavy rain but that you do want to get wet. What might you do to get completely drenched?"

The youth might hold out their arms and face the heavens; they might remove a jacket or a cap.

Say: "If you're stuck in a heavy rain, you're going to get wet. You can try to huddle up and stay dry, even though staying dry is impossible. Or you can open your arms and let the rain fall all over you. God's grace works in much the same way. God gives us grace no matter what. Means of grace—prayer, worship, Bible study, service, Holy Communion, and so forth—are the ways in which we open our arms and let God's grace drench us."

In the interest of getting the youth drenched with grace, ask them to look at the "Weekly Challenge" on page 28 of the student book (to commit to a daily time of prayer and devotion or to add a new spiritual practice to their daily routine).

Three Simple Rules 24/7

Without Ceasing?

Dim the lights and, if possible, use candlelight. If you have brought pillows, scatter them on the floor for the youth to sit on. Ask a youth to read aloud 1 Thessalonians 5:16-22, which is printed on page 27 of the student book.

Say: "Some Christians, particularly those in the Eastern Orthodox tradition, have taken very seriously Paul's command in 1 Thessalonians to 'pray without ceasing.' To be faithful to this command, many of these believers repeatedly say a prayer known as the Jesus Prayer or the Prayer of the Heart."

Supplies
- Candles (optional)
- Large, comfortable pillows scattered around the room (optional)

Tell the youth that the Jesus Prayer is printed at the bottom of page 27 of the student book. Explain that the key to the Jesus prayer is rhythm. One prays the first line as he or she inhales and the second line as he or she exhales:

Breathe in: Lord Jesus Christ, Son of God,
Breathe out: Have mercy on me, a sinner.

In this way, one breathes in the presence of Christ and breathes out a confession of one's sins. Explain that people who say the Jesus Prayer as a spiritual discipline start out by saying the prayer aloud or by moving their lips. They pray the prayer over and over again until they can shut out all distractions and focus on God. Then they continue repeating the prayer, this time mentally. Eventually, the prayer moves from the head to the heart; and they pray without having to think about doing so. The prayer becomes as natural as breathing.

Those who are able to pray the Jesus Prayer "without ceasing" often report feeling closer to God, being more aware of God's presence, and having a more loving and forgiving attitude toward their fellow human beings.

Dim the lights, or if possible use candlelight. Invite the youth to find a comfortable place to sit and instruct everyone to be silent and close their eyes. Ask the youth to pray the Jesus Prayer, silently but moving their lips, over and over in rhythm with their breathing. Allow them to continue praying like this for the remainder of your time together.

Rule 3: Stay in Love With God

Reading Assignment (Optional)

If each youth has a copy of *Three Simple Rules,* by Rueben Job, ask them in the coming week to read the chapter "Stay in Love With God" (pages 53–63). Tell them to think about the following questions as they read. (These are printed on page 30 of the student book).

- What is most challenging about following this rule to "stay in love with God" (or as Wesley said, "attend upon all the ordinances of God")?
- How is this rule similar to and different from the first two rules?
- In what ways do you show your love for God?
- What practices could you take on that would bring you closer to God?
- How would being fully devoted to following this rule change your attitude and behavior? How would it help you practice the first two rules?
- How would your church, your community, and our nation be different if everyone were to take this rule seriously?

Session

Rule 3: Stay in Love With God
Part 2

Theme: Staying in love with God, in practice

Key Scripture: "Simon, son of John, do you love me more than these?" [Simon Peter] said to him, "Yes, Lord; you know that I love you." Jesus said to him, "Feed my lambs" (John 21:15).

Without Ceasing (Reprise)

Before the youth arrive, dim the lights in your meeting space and, if possible, use candlelight. If you have brought pillows, scatter them on the floor for the youth to sit on. Write on a markerboard the following instructions:

Supplies
- Candles (optional)
- Large, comfortable pillows scattered around the room (optional)

Spend five minutes in silence, praying the Jesus Prayer:

Breathe in: Lord Jesus Christ, Son of God,
Breathe out: Have mercy on me, a sinner.

As the youth arrive, point to the markerboard. (If some youth were not present for the previous session, quietly explain the Jesus Prayer to them.) Allow the youth about five minutes to quietly pray the Jesus Prayer. Then ask:

- What thoughts or feelings did you experience as you were praying?
- Did the prayer fall into rhythm with your breathing? Did it take on a life of its own?
- How might this type of prayer bring you closer to God? How might it affect your attitude toward others?

Then ask the youth how they fared with the previous week's "Weekly Challenge" (to commit to a daily time of prayer and devotion or to add a new spiritual practice to their daily routine). Ask them what was most difficult and most worthwhile about taking on this prayer time or spiritual practice, and encourage them to continue developing these habits.

Rule 3: Stay in Love With God

Reading Assignment (Optional)

If your group did the optional reading assignment (the "Stay in Love With God" chapter of *Three Simple Rules*), open by asking the youth to give their impressions of the reading and to name some of the key points that author Rueben Job makes in this chapter. Then discuss the questions below (page 30 of the student book), which the youth were asked to reflect on:

- What is most challenging about practicing this rule to "stay in love with God" (or as Wesley said, "attend upon all the ordinances of God")?
- How is this rule similar to and different from the first two rules?
- In what ways do you show your love for God?
- What practices could you take on that would bring you closer to God?
- How would being fully devoted to following this rule change your attitude and behavior? How would it help you follow the first two rules?
- How would your church, your community, and our nation be different if everyone were to take this rule seriously?

Getting Out More

Ask a youth to read aloud the excerpt from *Three Simple Rules* printed on page 31 of the student book. The youth should remember this excerpt, with deals with inside-out living, from the previous session.

Say: "Spiritual disciplines bring us closer to God and enrich our hearts and souls; but they also affect our attitudes, behaviors, and relationships with others. This is the 'out' part of inside-out living."

One reason that many people today struggle to faithfully practice spiritual disciplines is that so many other things compete for their attention. People today have so many things to do, watch, play, listen to, and buy; and advertisers work hard to remind people of all of these options. With that in mind, challenge the youth to create an advertising campaign for a spiritual discipline.

Divide the youth into teams of 3 or 4, and instruct each team to come up with an ad campaign to convince people to engage in a certain spiritual practice. Encourage the teams to think of a variety of ways to advertise these disciplines, using a variety of media (television, Internet, billboards, word of mouth, and so forth). Suggest that they use their campaigns to lift up the benefits of the practices that they are advertising.

Give the youth several minutes to work, then allow each team to present (or "pitch") its campaign. After each presentation, ask:

- What was the strongest part of this advertising campaign? What about this campaign makes you want to do the practice being advertised?

After all of the teams have had a chance to present, ask:

- Can you advertise spiritual practices in the same way that people advertise cars, shoes, or hamburgers? Why, or why not?
- In what ways do people learn the value of spiritual practices such as prayer, worship, service, and Bible study? (*from the testimony of others, by seeing how these practices change people's lives, through a desire to grow closer to God*)
- How difficult is it to devote time to these spiritual practices, when so many other things clamor for your attention? What sorts of things distract you from your relationship with God?
- How can you eliminate distractions and draw closer to God through prayer and other spiritual practices?

24/7 Holiness

Ask a volunteer to read aloud the excerpt from *Three Simple Rules* printed on page 31 of the student book. This excerpt suggests that staying in love with God involves more than just the spiritual practices that John Wesley named (prayer, worship, Holy Communion, Bible study, and fasting), that it involves other spiritual practices such as providing for the needs of others.

Explain that there is no list of official spiritual practices and no limits to the ways in which we can stay in love with God. Suggest that we can show our love for God by serving others, standing up for those who are powerless, caring for creation, praising God through music and other arts, and using spiritual discernment when making choices.

Divide youth into groups of 3 or 4, and challenge each group to make a list of ways in which they can stay in love with God in their daily lives.

Rule 3: Stay in Love With God

Give the teams two minutes to make their lists, then invite each team to read aloud its list. After each item is read have members of the other groups raise their hands if they had listed the same item. Have the groups cross out any items that another group had listed so that only the unique items remain. See which group listed the most unique examples of staying in love with God. You might award a prize to the winning team. (This activity is very similar to "Proactive Goodness," on pages 24–25.)

Then give the youth about five minutes to work individually to complete "24/7 Holiness" on page 31 of the student book. In this activity, the students will identify the spiritual practice named in each of several Scriptures. As time permits, allow volunteers to name the spiritual practices that they identified.

Feeding Lambs

If possible, arrange beforehand for a guest speaker from your congregation to talk with your youth about one way in which your congregation feeds Jesus' "sheep." This could be a ministry that feeds the hungry, helps people overcome addiction, fights for affordable housing in your community, or does something else to meet the needs of people locally or globally.

Say: "During the Last Supper, Jesus predicted that his disciple Peter would deny him three times. Peter vowed he would do no such thing."

Ask a volunteer to read aloud Matthew 26:69-75, in which Jesus' prediction comes true as Peter denies his teacher three times. Tell the youth that Peter's denials are not the end of the story.

Ask volunteers to read aloud John 21:15-19, each person reading a verse at a time from a Bible. Point out that Jesus asks Peter, "Do you love me?" three times, once for each of Peter's denials. Then ask:

- When Peter tells Jesus that he loves him, how does Jesus respond? (*"Feed my lambs"; "Tend my sheep"; and "Feed my sheep."*)
- Who are Jesus' sheep? (*Those who follow him.*)

Say: "Jesus essentially tells Peter that staying in love with God involves loving God's children by meeting their needs. 'Feeding God's sheep' can involve tending to someone's physical needs by offering food or shelter; it can also involve tending to someone's spiritual needs by praying together or offering a listening ear."

Three Simple Rules 24/7

Ask the youth to brainstorm a list of ways that your congregation feeds God's sheep.

Then introduce your guest speaker. Ask this person to talk about the ministry that he or she is involved in, how this ministry feeds God's sheep (whether physically, spiritually, or both), and how the youth could get involved in this ministry. Allow time for the youth to ask questions.

Into the World With Three Simple Rules

Hand out index cards, and invite the youth to think about the three simple rules they've been focusing on in this study: Do no harm, do good, and stay in love with God.

Supplies
- Index cards
- Bulletin board and pushpins, or tape

Instruct the youth to turn to the final page in their student book. Give them about five minutes to come up with one way in which they will practice each of these three simple rules on an ongoing basis in the coming days, weeks, months, and years. Tell the youth that the commitments they make should be specific, achievable, and relevant to their lives.

Instruct the youth to write down these commitments both in the space provided in the student book and on their index cards. Let the students know that their classmates will be reading what they write.

After five minutes, invite the youth to pin their cards to a bulletin board or tape them to a wall. Encourage the youth, as they return to this space in the future (whether for Sunday school, youth group, Bible study, or something else), to look back at the commitments they have made and to ask their classmates how they have been doing with these commitments. Explain that holding one another accountable to the vows we make is an important part of living in Christian community.

Three Simple Rules

Intergenerational Worship

As you study *Three Simple Rules 24/7: A Wesleyan Way of Living,* by Rueben P. Job, with the youth, children, and adults of your congregation, you may want to plan for group involvement in intergenerational activities. Consider these possibilities:

- Plan a concluding celebration on a Sunday morning that will create a renewed commitment to practicing the three simple rules. Recruit adults, youth, and children to offer testimonies about what they learned and practiced during their study.

- Add an intergenerational activity to each session. For example, the combined group might create a group banner for each of the three simple rules. The banners can then be displayed in the sanctuary during the a worship service as a reminder of what the groups have learned.

- Make suggestions of songs or hymns that reflect the three simple rules for those who plan the worship services for the weeks following the study. Have someone name the connections to the three simple rules when the songs are sung.

- Prepare a video or skits that illustrate the three simple rules. Involve actors from all age groups.

- Have children, youth, and adults work together to design the worship altar that reflects the meanings of the three simple rules in the lives of Christians.

Notes